"NURSE!"
"Yes, Sister?"

Dorothy Gill

"NURSE!"
"Yes, Sister?"

Dorothy Gill

ATHENA PRESS
LONDON

"NURSE!"
"Yes, Sister?"
Copyright © Dorothy Gill 2004

All Rights Reserved

No part of this book may be reproduced in any form
by photocopying or by any electronic or mechanical means,
including information storage or retrieval systems,
without permission in writing from both the copyright
owner and the publisher of this book.

ISBN 1 84401 367 7

First Published 2004 by
ATHENA PRESS
Queen's House, 2 Holly Road
Twickenham, TW1 4EG
United Kingdom

Printed for Athena Press

*Dedicated to the many hospital matrons of old,
who were the real essence of nursing.
They oversaw the housing, cleaning, laundering, feeding, physical
and mental caring of patients and staff alike.
They earned respect and gave respect as they carried and passed on
"the lamp".
Their demise has not been without effect.*

Contents

INTRODUCTION	xi
CHAPTER I	
In the Beginning, Summer 1949	13
CHAPTER II	
Preliminary Training	18
CHAPTER III	
The End of the Beginning	27
CHAPTER IV	
First Allocation	30
CHAPTER V	
Feeling the Pain	36
CHAPTER VI	
Time Passing	43
CHAPTER VII	
Nursing the Sick Children	44
CHAPTER VIII	
Nursing Patients with Pulmonary Tuberculosis	48
CHAPTER IX	
Operating Theatre	52
CHAPTER X	
Female Surgical Nursing	56

CHAPTER XI
Social Life during Training 63

CHAPTER XII
Classroom Days 66

CHAPTER XIII
Night Duty in the Smog of '52 69

CHAPTER XIV
Casualty and Out Patients 71

CHAPTER XV
Nursing the Sick Babies 75

COMPLETION 77

INTRODUCTION

IT IS UNDENIABLE THAT WHEN THE FOCUS OF NURSES' training moved from a practical base with a deep theoretical understanding, to that of a theoretical research base, much of the quality hands-on care was lost to the patient. The apprenticeship skills-based training which had evolved over many decades in various schools of nursing attached to their mother hospitals was the envy of many a country throughout the world, whether of ancient or modern history.

Our registered nurses were coveted worldwide, yet paradoxically never valued by the State for their input to the nation's health or wealth. Many of these well-trained persons during the Sixties and Seventies went abroad where they were eagerly accepted, and in most cases well recompensed. With a change in approach to giving nursing care in a markedly different ethos in hospitals as a whole and nurses moving more and more into the realm of doctoring, one is left wondering, who is going to meet the basic needs of the patient?

This book is a short account of my nurse-training memories, written to remind me of how things were, when nothing came easy for the patients we cared for, when we tried to make the best of a hard job and delighted in our place in the scheme of things.

CHAPTER I

In the Beginning,
SUMMER 1949

SHE SAT BEHIND A HEAVY MAHOGANY DESK, WEARING a navy blue, thick fabric dress; around the upstanding collar and at the wrist of the long sleeves were tiny white linen bands. On her head was a white cap simply frilled, allowing only a few wisps of hair to be visible on the forehead, behind the ears and at the nape of the neck. She had a kindly pink face and a quiet, soft-spoken manner. This was Matron.

Mother and I sat across the desk, quite overawed by the environment we found ourselves in, but we were put at ease by her welcome. I handed over my school reports. These were minimal as my schooling had been interrupted twice by being sent to Devon as an evacuee. The tiny village school had tried to cope with the huge influx of very sparky East-End evacuees. My age of seventeen years was verified on my birth certificate. A few questions were asked about why I had chosen nursing as a career. At this time work opportunities were limited to the "rag trade", factory or shop work. Horizons were not yet broad for East End youth, trade and industry still labouring under the aftermath of the war.

In answer to Matron's questions I said that I had been influenced mainly by a friend of the family, a young lady who was already at the end of her nurse training. She had told me it was hard but rewarding work.

Mother and I seemed to be sitting stiff-backed in our

"NURSE!"
"Yes, Sister?"

chairs. Matron outlined the three years of training and explained I would have an extra year to complete as the final examinations could only be taken after reaching twenty-one years of age. A list of necessities that I would need to start would be sent to me, she said, if I decided to accept the place in training she was offering.

I could not believe her words. "Yes please," was my reply. It all seemed so calm and simple. I was going to be a nurse. I would start training in three months – October 1949.

Some days later I received a letter from Matron: instructions as to date and time to arrive; to whom to report and where to find her. This was to be Home Sister, and she became a guiding light in the first exciting days. Also enclosed was a document listing the items I would need initially:

- Black flat/Cuban-heeled, laced shoes;
- Shoe-cleaning material;
- Black stockings;
- White hair grips;
- Note-taking material;
- Coloured pencils.

I was to return to Matron's office a further document with various dress-size measurements, so that my uniform would be ready for my arrival. This document I returned post haste. In these few weeks waiting I started practising anatomical drawings of bones and muscles and pored over Father's *Pears Encyclopaedia of Family Medicine*.

October 1949 arrived. All newcomers had been asked to arrive by late afternoon. I recall entering the door to the hospital. It was not in the least bit imposing. Up two steps and through another pair of doors, and there before me stretched a corridor as far as the eye could see. The length was covered with terrazzo flooring. Tall windows ran down

"NURSE!"
"Yes, Sister?"

each side from beginning to end. I breathed in the then typical hospital smell. This, then, was St Andrews, founded in 1868 as the Poplar and Stepney Sick Asylum, built and opened in 1873 and where a school of nursing was founded in 1875. It was surrounded on all sides by cleared bomb sites. What an amazing escape for the old building.

I made my way to Home Sister's office, with knees knocking and hands trembling, and introduced myself. She was a magisterial figure in the same navy uniform with white trim as I had seen on Matron, but she put me at ease and made me feel as though I was expected. Already some newcomers were in residence, having arrived early on the boat-train from Ireland. Some of them were red-eyed from weeping and lonely for home, so I felt I was not too badly off.

The nurses' home was in two sections, called the old and the new home. Four to five stories high, it was a complex of high-ceilinged dark corridors in the "old" home and more spacious and airy in the "new". Both buildings had convolutions of staircases and seemed eerily silent.

My first impression on being taken to my room was of the gloom. High ceilings in the corridors and small light bulbs hanging high did little to bring light or cheer. The walls were of a dark olive green on the bottom half and a dark beige/cream on the top half. The floor was, as in the main hospital corridor, a muted mix of terrazzo. Sister opened the door to my room; old home, first floor, second room on the left after ascending from Home Sister's office. She handed me the keys. The room was high-ceilinged and dark. It had a window which looked out upon the roofs of lower hospital buildings; all coated with the grime and soot from home and factory chimneys and of the fires from the bombing.

The room had a tiny cast-iron fireplace, unused for many years. The flooring was a very dark green rubberised

"NURSE!"
"Yes, Sister?"

material and the walls were the same beige/cream as in the corridors. It was furnished with a black-painted iron bedstead. The bed was made up; alongside it was a small locker, and also in the room was a small dressing table, chair and wardrobe. It was sparse but waxy smelling clean, and coming from a bedroom shared by three sisters this was a palace, but a non-starter by today's standards.

On the bed was a bundle; tied up were my uniform dresses, Sister Dora caps, linen bag and record book.

I was amazed at the organisation that had resulted from the little document on which I had months previously written and returned the requested measurements. Each dress had a label with my name stitched onto it, likewise the caps and bag. At this point I felt I was really part and parcel of this, to my untutored eye, vast hospital organisation.

Home Sister had said to meet up with the other girls on the corridor, to try on uniforms together, to make up and fit on our Sister Dora caps, and that someone would collect us later and take us to the dining room for supper. So we met up, all feeling very strange but all in the same boat. We giggled and laughed as we tried on these not vary glamorous coat/dress uniforms and puzzled our way around the Sister Dora caps. The strongest impression of those first hours was that this organisation was prepared for our coming. All our uniforms were ready and I had my name on a door to a room and I had a key and this was my own living space; and if the apparent camaraderie of the initial few hours was anything to go by, it looked as though our training together would be enjoyable. It was all down to me to fit in.

As promised, a student nurse came to take us to the dining room, explaining as we went a few dos and don'ts. Through passageways and doors we eventually reached the dining room. It was a large, bright room with shining parquet flooring. Places were designated for students, trained staff and other professionals. We queued up and

"NURSE!"
"Yes, Sister?"

were issued with a labelled jam jar in which was a measure of butter; this was our ration for the week. It was to be stored for our own use in a cupboard in the dining room; we were still suffering rationing in the post-war era.

After the meal it was back to our rooms to ready ourselves for the next day and the start of our training…

CHAPTER II
Preliminary Training

THE FIRST TWELVE WEEKS OF TRAINING WERE TO BE spent on the study of the theory and practice of nursing and its many allied subjects – bacteriology, first aid, hygiene, anatomy and physiology, nutrition and sickroom cookery. Our base was in a classroom; a ward converted with the usual classroom equipment at one end and at the other a fairly typical bedside area, with two beds, ward furniture and many cupboards of equipment. Thirty young women started training on this date, two English and twenty eight Irish. Sister Tutor was a flame-haired Irish woman who would accept only the best work possible from all of us, and was pretty fearsome in approach, but eventually won the love and respect of her new brood.

On the first morning we all turned up in our white twill dresses, which buttoned on the shoulder and down the side – not very glamorous; very much designed for utility and efficiency. Sister Dora caps were on our heads at various angles, with hair scragged and clipped back underneath. Pens were in pockets, also the obligatory round-ended scissors. We were all fresh-faced and eager to start.

The first hours were a heavy concentration of guidelines from Sister Tutor. Class times were from eight to five thirty and on a Saturday from eight to one. A list of topics to be covered was given to us and we were told a weekly test would be set for each Saturday morning and each paper had to have a pass mark.

Personal care and hygiene was a prime topic. Clean,

"NURSE!"
"Yes, Sister?"

short hair up off the collar was a necessity to prevent our dust and bacteria shedding down onto the patient. Nails were to be short and no nail varnish – this was often checked on. No rings or necklaces or earrings to limit the risk of a patient being scratched or indeed the patient grabbing the jewellery and harming the nurse; the jewellery could also harbour bacteria. A daily bath was advised. Towels and hot water were available, so there was no excuse for not conforming. Black stockings and black, clean shoes were to be worn, ideally laced up to support the foot bones and arches; vital when we were to be on our feet for many hours of the day. Uniform was never to be worn out of the hospital and sitting on beds was forbidden. Hands were to be washed and dried after every procedure, and especially when moving on to another patient. Those first talks gave us much food for thought.

In the first induction days, one by one we each attended Home Sister in the clinical room, for weighing and height measurement and a general health history. The staff doctor, the senior hospital physician, gave each student a full health check. A Mantoux test was given to assess our susceptibility to pulmonary tuberculosis. Monitoring of our weight and well-being throughout our training was done annually, and Home Sister was always available if we had a problem or needed to report sick.

After the preliminaries we really got down to work. The school day started with us scouring the classroom, especially the area laid out as a ward. A daily domestic cleaning lady dealt with the floor, which was shining parquet, and cleansed the annexes. She had worked in the hospital for many years and was finalising her service in the relatively easy environment of the schoolroom; she was a very kindly old soul to us newcomers. Daily we damp dusted everything in sight. High dusting on long, long handles was done less frequently. Daily we washed bedpans and urinals

"NURSE!"
"Yes, Sister?"

and washed and powdered red rubber mackintoshes, these being used to protect the mattresses. All this activity inculcated in us the need for cleanliness and familiarised us with the equipment we were going to meet in the real sickroom.

We were taught techniques of ventilating the ward so as not to create a draught, being taught the differences between convection and radiation currents in relation to heating; reading and recording the temperature under the watchful eye of Sister Tutor; checking supplies; learning what to order and from whom and then checking the order in later; and learning the names of the weird and wonderful equipment and its uses. It was an Aladdin's cave to the unknowing; this was just the start of the day.

After returning from a coffee break of half an hour, during which time we also had to get to our rooms to make our beds and tidy up, we started lectures covering first aid, personal and nursing hygiene, nutrition and anatomy, and physiology and bacteriology. During the first week a bookseller came to demonstrate his wares and we were advised as to the best purchases for our needs by Sister Tutor, each one of us being restricted by having very little cash. So we bought what we could, and with Sister Tutor's lessons we started absorbing information like thirsty sponges.

Following lunch we were given the theories behind basic nursing practises, such as simply putting a pleat into the sheet over the patient's toes, thus preventing pressure on the heels where pressure sores could develop, as patients were in bed for weeks on end; on the positioning of pillows in a specific way to allow for improved breathing, and the use of the bed table on which the patient could lean, arms akimbo, to fix the shoulder girdle – once again to help with breathing.

There were times the classroom echoed with laughter; as

"NURSE!"
"Yes, Sister?"

with the practising of bed bathing a patient, Mrs Kelly, the life-sized doll. She suffered greatly at our hands, and our hilarity was soon called to order. We eventually advanced to the stage of using a class member in a swimsuit. We were shown carefully how to cross arms and legs to turn the patient onto the side, supporting the head as the pillow was repositioned then carefully rolling in under the previously prepared draw sheet and red rubber mackintosh, pulling it taut, with the reserve tucked in and ready for later use. There was a reasoned explanation for all actions and every movement. The straightforward making of an empty bed speedily was demonstrated by the footwork and handwork of the nurses on each side of the bed working in complete unison; it saved so much effort and energy.

All the equipment necessary for each separate procedure had to be learned, and before any was used it had to be checked beforehand. Forgetting an item once the task was started was frowned upon. The constantly telling the patient what you were doing was a must and had to continue at each phase of care, however self-conscious one felt talking to a life-sized manikin. The practice area was a hive of industry in the afternoons with Sister Tutor demonstrating with a helper, then each getting practice, while groups were spread around the room practising bandaging, looking at bones and practising resuscitation after drowning.

We practised on each other the methods of taking the temperature, pulse and respiration, diligently counting the seconds, and noted the changes after running on the spot and touching toes with varying degrees of vigour. Few of us had a watch with a second hand, so we used a small instrument called a pulsometer. It was like a miniature egg-timer; indeed, later in training we *did* use them as egg-timers. To complete the practice we had to record our personal readings on a chart and maintain this during the schooling period, so too observations of urine, noting the

"NURSE!"
"Yes, Sister?"

normal and abnormal. Laboratory-style urine glasses were filled with specimens obtained from adjacent wards. These were inspected and Sister Tutor demonstrated, using chemical reagents, the presence of sugar, acetone, blood and so on with a small glass methylated spirit lamp and test tubes. We boiled and bubbled away at the specimens, being made acutely aware of how important our accurate testing would be to the well-being of the patient.

Towards the end of the day we sat at vast tables, we were glad to rest our legs. There we practised making "tow curls", tow being a very coarse "coir"-type fibre. It was firstly picked over to remove the very coarsest fibres, then stranded around the fingers. The little ball-like curls were used to wipe a patient after using the bed pan. Not for them the soft wipes of today.

During other sessions we pored over skeletal specimens, learning the notches and the ridges, holes and bumps on all the bones, referring to charts and books as we did so. Another task for each student was to pad a wooden splint; there were only two ways to do it – a right way and a wrong way. This entailed layers of tow and non-absorbent wool being positioned on a wooden slab 8" x 3" x ½", over this was laid linen. This cushion of fabrics then had to be stitched in a quite specific way, each stitch size and type had to be sewn meticulously or it was not acceptable. The non-sewers or ham-fisted found it hard going. On completion the splints were sent to the casualty department where they were in great demand. Not for us a plastic cock-up splint!

Lessons carried on, day in day out. Mostly we absorbed it all like sponges, but we were getting anxious to see "real" patients and practise our skills. Hygiene was a subject which permeated every aspect of care, both personal and patient. On one well remembered occasion our brilliant Sister Tutor linked personal hygiene and hospital economy. She described how the old order was changing and that since 1948 the National Health Service had come into being.

"NURSE!"
"Yes, Sister?"

"A service to be funded by the country's workers," she said, "in the form of National Insurance and Taxation."

All were entitled to use this service, regardless of colour, creed or social class. She strutted around the classroom; we were all wrapt in attention. "How many pieces, I repeat, how many pieces of toilet paper do you use when in the toilet?" A stunned silence and an intake of breath by all of us now agog.

"Remember, remember," she said, "this is not a free service; nothing is free, the people are paying for every item you use, therefore do not waste anything, however insignificant it may seem."

It was a stern lesson, which I think we registered at the time, but still the hygiene lesson continued. We donned our scarlet-lined, navy blue capes and went outside into the chill air. We were directed to look up and observe the many pipes that were affixed to the wall of the nurses' home; we noted the diameters, the angles and various configurations, we noted the soil pipes and air vents and were told of the function of each. A member of the hospital engineering team appeared and lifted drain and manhole covers, pointing out glazings, gullies and traps and what each did. We came into the classroom chilled but more aware of our environment, and inspected in detail the case of miniaturised earthenware-glazed models of drainage equipment, toilets and sluices too. The whole lesson was rounded off with a film from the Central Office of Information entitled *Taken for Granted*. It showed the treatment of all waste from its many sources – homes, factories, institutions and roads – through the total treatments in use at the time to the production of water to be used again at taps, toilets and so on. It was an intensely interesting session, which drew many threads together. Later in the year we were taken to the waterworks shown in the film, and this further consolidated the information.

"NURSE!"
"Yes, Sister?"

How to feed patients in various stages of illness was a vital part of our primary course, so with a basic grounding in nutritional needs having been learnt from lectures, we set off for a number of sessions in the hospital kitchens. These took place late in the afternoons, after all meals had been cooked.

The kitchens were huge, with red quarry-tiled floors and glass roofs, giant hotplates of stainless steel with ovens below, vats for making and storing soups lined the walls. Being closely monitored by Sister Tutor we chopped up beef that was placed in cool-boiled water; this was to be "beef tea". We were taught the niceties of coddling eggs and using rennet to make blancmange. Favourite by far was the egg-nog mixture with frothy egg white on top. Delicate sandwiches were made with great care. Nothing was wasted in those days of food scarcity; the prepared food from our lessons all went off to the deserving on the wards. How to present foods was practised in the schoolroom. Using trays and tray cloths we set for various meals, being advised that the only time a nurse sat at the patient's bedside was when feeding a patient. There were quite a few coughs and splutters as we practised our skills using a spouted feeding cup, but better to practise on the fit and healthy than a really sick patient.

Friday of each week was full of trepidation. Continuing our training depended on passing our weekly test. We were given papers with questions relating to the topics covered during the week, and often an anatomical drawing was called for. Papers were marked and returned as early as the following week, and as with any testing/examination situation, the further into the course one advanced the greater the apprehension. The final examination in the preliminary course also had an element of display of practical skills and knowledge, so we spent a lot of time, off duty too, scurrying around practising our bedside skills.

"NURSE!"
"Yes, Sister?"

So the days went by, the classroom and annexes always shining as a result of our daily scrubbing and polishing. Sister Tutor kept a close watch on our hands and hair, shoes and stockings; no standard was allowed to slip. With our increasing assurance and knowledge of anatomy and physiology and the equipment we used and with the understanding of the rationale behind the use we practised our new skills on each other. Bending knees, straightening backs we moved in unison at the bedside. We bed bathed, washed hair, cleansed mouths. We lifted, log-rolled, positioned for examination our guinea-pig colleagues, with hilarity on occasion but an ever present awareness of the seriousness of our actions.

It was a muted group that gathered when the timetable showed the topic to be "The laying out of the dead". Laying out the dead and the care of the relatives was treated with great solemnity. We were made aware of varying religious practises in relation to the dead, each patient having on the front of his medical notes a clearly-indicated, brightly-coloured sticker. For this lesson we were all allowed to sit in a semi-circle around the bed enclosed with screens. Sister Tutor was assisted in the task of preparing the body by one of the students, selected because they had already been present at a death, whereas the majority of us had not.

The lesson was concluded with a discussion on removing the body from the ward and escorting it to the mortuary, further reinforced by a visit to the mortuary and the chapel of rest and being shown the facilities for the deceased and the relatives. It was a very sombre group that finished the day.

During the weeks of the preliminary course we had discussions with the clergymen of the main faiths, which at the time were: Church of England; Roman Catholic; Jewish and Non-Conformist. The knowledge of our society as a whole was broadened, and our awareness of the needs of all

"NURSE!"
"Yes, Sister?"

groups was developed. It was not until much later in my training that further different clergy had to be sent for as the patients being admitted were becoming more and more multi-national and multi-faith. It was stressed frequently during our hectic bedside nursing theory and practice that we were caring not only for the patient's physical and mental needs but also the spiritual.

As student nurses we were taught that running, except in the case of haemorrhage or fire, was not acceptable. We were taught to move smoothly, swiftly and quietly at all times.

Emergency fire drill was quite exciting. The hospital fire officer came and discussed dealing with a fire emergency and the very important dos and don'ts. We toured with him a number of hospital sites, looking at the fire escapes, alarms and fire exits, pointing out potential hazards as we went, even to the point of someone breaking the glass to set all alarm bells ringing. Every move was detailed as to the actions to be taken on the discovery of a fire, with a number of "what if" scenarios being explained. Emergency fireman's lifts were practised, with stress being put on the incapacitated patients and their movement to places of safety.

The session culminated outside the schoolroom using fire extinguishers, where with much laughter we drenched each other as we learnt the handling of the cumbersome appliances. Annual attendance at a fire drill was compulsory throughout training and after for all staff.

CHAPTER III
The End of the Beginning

AT THE END OF EACH DAY WE FINISHED QUITE TIRED and we wearily went to our rooms, little knowing the tiredness to come when working in the real hospital environment. Generally we chatted over our day's experiences. When refreshed we gathered together in groups sitting on beds and floors, swotting up on our notes, using question and answer sessions often broken up with roars of laughter at someone's witticism.

There were no distractions like TV or radio; they were not part of everyday life. The only radio was in the huge sitting room on the ground floor, and we hadn't yet ventured from our own cliques to mix with more senior status nurses. Social life was nonexistent; we had no cash and had to wait a full month before we all trooped to the boardroom on the main corridor, formed a queue, and under the eagle eye of the deputy matron signed on the dotted line for our first meagre pay packet. We were then handed by the finance officer a brown envelope. For the first year it was the princely sum of two hundred and twenty-five pounds, minus a deduction of a hundred and eight pounds for board and lodgings, which gave us nine pounds and a few pence per month. The brown envelope was not bursting at the seams.

The social scene for student nurses was very simple, especially in the first months. We were in a very strange, protective and different world, and in comparison with today's eighteen/nineteen-year-olds we were not very

"NURSE!"
"Yes, Sister?"

worldly wise. Outside of the hospital environment too the morals were very different, but we stuck together and gradually started coming out of our shells. Facilities provided by the hospital authorities for our entertainment were: table tennis; a radiogram in the sitting room; and two weed-covered hard tennis courts. The days being long with so much swotting to do, we were not overly concerned. Sometimes we did play 78 rpm records at full blast and danced like demons, and on more than one occasion irate senior nurses descended to the sitting room to ask us to hush.

House rules demanded that we kept our rooms tidy; beds had to be made according to the hospital pattern. The rooms were swept and polished by the cleaning ladies, who were usually elderly. They took a great pride in their work and were very much mother figures to us all, especially to those a long way from home. The nurse's homes were formally inspected every month by a retinue of Matron or Deputy Matron and Home Sister. No nook or cranny was left free from their piercing eyes. These experienced nurses were up to all the tricks!

And so our twelve weeks of preliminary training were coming to an end. We were a very different group of girls from the unknowing gaggle of females that had entered the school. We knew we could perform the basic skills, but the fear of the unknown situation was present in all of us. We had heard many tales from our predecessors about the work on the wards and circumstances we would most commonly meet and the dos and don'ts relative to them.

A ward or department allocation was of three-month duration and a "change list" was posted up outside the dining room. Many were the oohs and aahs from the fledgling nurses as they scanned the list. Some areas of work were as notorious as some of the sisters. It happened that my first allocation was to a male medical ward, the ward

"NURSE!"
"Yes, Sister?"

sister of which had a fearsome reputation for being a hard taskmaster, so I was full of trepidation, being concerned by my lack of years and "street cred". The worry, however, was not justified, as it turned out. In the week before our leaving school it was our duty to report to our wards of allocation. The greetings were warm and welcoming. Off duty was explained and information in reporting on and off duty and requests for study times and other possible absences were outlined.

Latterly in our course Matron attended the schoolroom and gave talks on the history and ethics of nursing. We were made very much aware of the regard in which the population held nurses and how to carry the lamp firmly and maintain always the highest standards. It was stressed that we were student nurses: the only person entitled to use the honoured title of "Nurse" was a registered nurse who had completed a course of training and was duty registered with the General Nursing Council. There were different registrations covering general, psychiatric and sick children groups.

With a degree of sadness we cleaned the sluices, bedsteads and everything cleanable to be ready for the next group to take over. We turned our chairs up on top of our desks, said farewell to our tutor, who had been a rock of support and professional guidance throughout, and left the preliminary schooling days of our training. It was coming up to Christmas 1949.

CHAPTER IV

First Allocation

THIS ALLOCATION MADE THE GREATEST IMPRESSION on me. Christmas was near and there was an undercurrent of excitement, much boosted by the active preparations of decorating the ward and annexes.

Ward staff consisted of Sister, Staff Nurse, a third-year nurse, a second-year – maybe even two: like the first years, it depended on the number at intake – there was often a state enrolled assistant nurse or one in the process of training for the roll. Each ward had its own "domestic" and ward orderly. Very often the domestic was a local lady of mature years and "her ward" was a place of great pride to her. The standards of work carried out were of the highest and no one liked to upset Mrs Green. She knew of every nook and cranny in the ward that she had cleaned over the years. There was an obvious mutual respect between Sister and her domestic. The ward orderly was younger and dealt with the lighter cleaning, dusting, sinks and kitchen work; they, like the domestics, enjoyed having their own ward and were much put out on having to be transferred in an emergency to another ward.

Early morning duties after hearing the night report started immediately. Initially much of what was said went over my head and there was no time for gossiping. Sister was conducted around by the night nurse and a word of greeting was given to each patient and any problems that had arisen were discussed. As the most junior student my first job was to collect all water jugs and glasses from the

"NURSE!"
"Yes, Sister?"

lockers and take them to the ward kitchen, to be washed and returned later when all locker tops had been cleaned. The ward was a hive of activity for the first few hours, possibly the busiest of the day: the domestic sprinkling damp tea-leaves before sweeping the floor; on certain days each week the beds were pulled to the centre from the walls so they could be thoroughly swept and mopped behind. On another day a heavy polishing bumper sitting on a pad of old blankets was swung to and fro, buffing in a wax polish, and the floors certainly gleamed. It was a cardinal sin to spill anything on the floor and not clean it up, but with all the toing and froing with jugs and bowls of hot water from the sink for washing and bathing the inevitable did happen. The banter amongst the domestic staff and the patients was very amusing; as staff and patients were locals they were very much on the same wavelength.

A not very pleasant task for the most junior was to collect the sputum mugs. They were mugs with a detachable flip-top lid made from a coated metal. Each mug had to have its contents observed before leaving the bedside for the presence of blood, pus or anything unusual, the various changes indicating certain diseases. After emptying the contents down the sluice, all the mugs had to be washed and dried. For this operation it was necessary to don a huge red rubber apron and gloves, these over the gown worn for the collection. The disinfectant used was called Sudol. With a smell akin to Creosote it came in a large container called a "Winchester", which held four pints. It was not an unpleasant smell but sufficient now to produce a déjà vu when someone is creosoting a fence. This task was carried out in a tiny space called the sluice annexe; the walls were hung with bed-pans and urinals. Contained within this small area was a rack hung with red rubber mackintoshes, the soiled linen carrier also. Two tiny cubicles, the male patients' toilets – of which there could be twenty-eight –

"NURSE!"
"Yes, Sister?"

were also sited in this area. One could almost feel it was a period of social exclusion while working there. But it was a vital job that had to be done. On completion a report was given to the nurse in charge and any suspect specimens observed by a senior and kept, labelled and seen by a doctor later.

Maintaining proper ventilation of the ward was a junior nurse's task, as was the recording of the ward temperature morning and evening. Pleasing all the patients was very difficult and we always ended up in someone's bad books. In the long Nightingale wards it was the practice to open alternate windows, never one facing, to avoid cross draughts.

Working alongside senior nurses the patients were bed-bathed. The equipment was prepared as near as possible as in the classroom; it was very good to put into practice the skills taught and learnt there. The rule was to work in pairs and the guidelines stressed the need for correct lifting and rolling, thus avoiding back strain on the nurses and injury to the patients. A man of fourteen stone was a different situation altogether from the manikin in the classroom, or indeed our colleagues who we had practiced on. At times we had to wait for help if we were working alone, but it was always wiser in the long run.

As the days went by I was now being able to relate the patient's specific diseases to the many and varied nursing bed positions we had been taught. For example, the positioning of pillows in a certain way for someone who was very breathless and the proper use of bed tables; noting the colour of the patient's skin, mucosa and nail beds; the degree of breathlessness, and at the same time learning the correct names – e.g. dyspnoea and orthopnoea – from this followed the administration of oxygen by various methods, with the warning that it was not unknown to find a patient having a quiet smoke alongside someone having oxygen.

"NURSE!"
"Yes, Sister?"

The patients, if at all possible, went home for Christmas, so the staff aimed to make the day as festive as possible for those remaining. These were very often suffering the long-term effects of harsh, damp, foggy London winters and exhausting working and living conditions not up to standard in the recently war-damaged city.

Streamers were put up and a little holly was put on the overhead lights. On Christmas day itself an extra large fire was stoked up at each end of the ward in the huge grates, which made it all so much more cheerful.

Christmas lunch was the main event of the day. All staff were on duty; no days off allowed. The hospital cooks excelled themselves with turkey and all the trimmings. Sister made as much of a ceremony of serving up the meal as possible and took great care, mince pies and Christmas puddings all part of it. For those who wished, a glass of stout was available, something Sister had hoarded for months. After lunch a cup of tea finished the meal, followed by a wash and tidy up, and then visitors were allowed in. The hours were extended but the rule still stood: only two visitors to each bed, though if children were involved the rule was bent for a few minutes as it was, after all, Christmas day. The visitors were very orderly, no one was allowed to sit on a bed but each bed had a stool or chairs.

Whilst the day was made special for the patients, Sister tried to make it special for her staff too. For the coffee break she had set out a delightful spread on the finest linen with delicate china and cutlery, and for each member of nursing staff she had exquisitely wrapped a little gift, mostly lacy and delicate which she had crafted herself. I remember my delight and disbelief that after being on the ward for only a few days she had a gift for me! After the stringent times of the war and still present rationing and hard times economically, this was a treat and gave insight as to how good things looked for the future.

"NURSE!"
"Yes, Sister?"

The nurses in turn went to lunch in the dining room whilst visitors were at the bedside. Our festive dinner was to be given in the weeks after Christmas. For the late afternoon Sister had organised a special tea, screened off in the corners of the ward whilst visitors were present. Whilst some were partaking, senior nurses patrolled the ward meeting patients' needs, chatting to visitors and patients. Staff from other areas called in with good wishes whilst doctors and other professionals came and went, sharing Christmas wishes with coffee, tea and Christmas treats.

And so the Christmas of 1949 came to an end. Winter was bringing its usual spate of severe chest infections. The smog was heavy, coal fires and factory chimney pollution continued unabated. The wards – especially the medical ones – were very busy.

Student nurses had one day off a week. The shifts were seven thirty a.m. start and finish at eight thirty p.m. and off duty for the day could be ten a.m. to one p.m. off duty, two p.m. to five p.m. off duty, or five p.m. off duty. There was little incentive to do anything other than rest and chat and swot the books. Although we were all teenagers the heavy, unusual physical and I suspect mental effort made us all somewhat weary; thoughts at that time did not turn to dancing and boyfriends, and the nearest one came to romance and sexuality was on the silver screen, and we didn't get to the cinema that often.

The grey, dark days of winter marched on. Each day we saw and learnt something new and began to grow in competence. One day going back following off duty and as was the norm reporting "on duty" to Sister in the office, she said, "Nurse, come with me."

We walked to the very end of the ward to the last bed on the left which was screened off. On the bed was a sheet-draped body. It was the first corpse I had ever seen. The gentleman was huge. Sister was small of stature and I was

"NURSE!"
"Yes, Sister?"

smaller. A trolley had been prepared and was alongside the bed, all the equipment for laying out the dead was on it. After explaining the procedure and stating the body had been left for one hour since death to rest, with much tenderness Sister quietly washed and dried the deceased with my assistance, explaining to me what she was doing and why, guiding me through every move, rolling and positioning gently and smoothly.

"Remember always," she said, "this could be your own kin." On completion my final nursing duty for the deceased was to escort him to the chapel of rest.

A porter came with a mortuary trolley. The body, with assistance from many other pairs of hands, was carefully put on the trolley; it was enclosed in a metal box-like cover and draped in a purple velvet pall. The other patients' beds were screened off. The body was then conducted to the mortuary chapel and handed over to the mortuary attendant.

CHAPTER V

Feeling the Pain

EQUIPMENT BY TODAY'S STANDARDS WAS MINIMAL and antiquated, but it was what we had and we cherished it. Syringes and needles were the most delicate and in short supply, therefore in frequent use.

Whilst on this, my first allocation, I had to develop my injection-giving skills. Fortunately not many drugs were administered in this way. The syringes were a glass barrel, metal nozzles and plunger. The ward stock consisted of something like four or five differing sizes. Needles were also few and far between and were of two sizes: one for a hypodermic injection and two for intramuscular injections. These very precious items of equipment after use were washed, then wrapped in a piece of old linen and placed in a receiver (kidney dish), which was usually of heavily chipped enamel, put into the ward steriliser and boiled for five minutes and were then ready for use again. The needles suffered greatly from the boiling, being battered on the enamel. In the classroom we had practiced on the manikin and a sponge ball, but inserting the needle into a real live patient made me feel queasy, and it was some time before I achieved a good dart technique for the intramuscular injections.

A new drug had just been introduced for the treatment of tuberculosis, this was Streptomycin. A young lad was admitted suffering form tubercular meningitis. The drug used to treat him was Streptomycin. It was not a pleasant task giving him an intramuscular injection into his buttock with such poor needles.

"NURSE!"
"Yes, Sister?"

This young lad was being barrier nursed, which was a method of creating an enclosure with screens, within the barrier the infected area. All equipment used in caring was marked, all washing and cleansing done within the barrier. Gowns were worn when caring and hands were thoroughly washed on entry and exit of the barrier. Observances of the techniques were stringent. Thankfully the outcome of this case was successful considering the dire situation.

The days were so busy. Up and down the ward, hustle and bustle. Voices always muted, patients dozing, and a few listening on the rare set of earphones to a ghastly crackle and pop set to music. Noise levels increased with the coming of patients' visitors, who were orderly and deferential in attitude. The major period of hush, however, was when the ward consultant did his rounds, usually once or twice a week. The ward was spic and span: all the patients eagerly waiting in their beds. Through the door came the great man with his retinue of registrars, housemen, physiotherapists, Sister and all the nurses, with the exception of those carrying on with essential nursing tasks. He passed from patient to patient with a few words to each, a few words to the registrar and often a sharp query to the housemen. Sister's expertise was often called upon.

"You'll learn a lot from Sister," he said to all, "heed her words."

Senior Nurse was responsible for making accurate notes of the changes in care ordered for each patient. X-rays were peered at, chests were percussed and listened to, and laboratory reports read. All the patients having been seen and encouraged, the great man moved to the ward sink where a specially pleated towel had been placed. Hands were washed and off into Sister's office accompanied by the registrar for a quick cup of tea, time permitting.

The ward livened up again. Many patients needed to have points clarified by the senior nurse as to what "he" had

"NURSE!"
"Yes, Sister?"

said, being so daunted by his presence at the time he was talking to them at the bedside. During the consultant's round, often taking two hours, essential nursing tasks continued: e.g. making observations and urine testing. There were many facets to the care of a patient with diabetes mellitus. There were many regimes of treatment in vogue. All food was weighed accurately in the ward kitchen, ounce by ounce. Urine had to be tested, often as frequently as every four hours; chemical reagents were used, and in one instance a test tube with "Benedict's" solution and urine was boiled to obtain the result. Then insulin had to be given by injection, amount according to the test reaction, and this was a task closely monitored by a senior nurse.

I remember being called to the bedside of a patient newly admitted in a ketonic coma. I was asked to smell the patient's breath. "What do you smell?" I was asked. It had a sweetish odour.

"New mown hay," said the senior. Then I remembered Sister Tutor's words: "Use all your senses when nursing to detect abnormalities," she had said. "Look, touch, smell and listen; the Egyptians called diabetes the sweet sickness, so they must have tasted the urine."

Staying with the diabetes theme, my task mid-morning was preparing a drink and biscuit in the kitchen for a patient. All the ward was busy. A hysterical nurse came to Sister at the office door and whispered in her ear, through the door they went with a tight-lipped sister saying, "Find me the 'Cheatles', Nurse." The situation was related to me later: a handsome young patient had responded amorously to the attractive nurses bed bathing him, Sister had had a word with him whilst holding the Cheatles; it had the desired effect and normality resumed.

From one patient to another we would go when practising taking pulses and listening to heartbeats, learning the differences between a dicrotic pulse and water hammer. It

"NURSE!"
"Yes, Sister?"

was our first use of the stethoscope as we listened to the heart's apex. One observation involved one nurse taking the pulse and one listening to the heart synchronising; this showed missed heartbeats. Another aspect was that the pulse rate was important when giving the drug Digitalis, which can slow the heart too much when administered over a long period. It was all really exciting, and the patients as well as the nurses were intrigued. They revelled in the listening to their own heartbeat through the stethoscope and could not do enough by offering their chests, wrists and necks to help our practise.

The use of bedding played a major role in nursing care. For example, we used a number of hot water bottles and many blankets; with the patient lying on a red rubber mackintosh and a blanket and covered by blankets, the hot water bottles were placed down either side of him, the blankets cocooned around him. This was part of the treatment to sweat a patient with nephritis.

Another common nursing technique was erecting a canopy over the bedhead using screens and sheets. An electric kettle with a very long spout which entered the canopy through a fold at the back was stood on a locker and plugged in. The steam produced created a humid atmosphere around the patient. This was used often in the case of patients with acute respiratory disease.

Bedheads and bed feet were lifted onto blocks for drainage of both limbs and lungs. Bending, stretching, lifting and walking we were as fit as fiddles as we learned our trade. Cleaning away equipment after use and leaving the bed-side tidy and clean was a must.

So the days ran into weeks, most days fairly routine. Patients in those days spent a lot of time in bed and weeks in hospital. Sunday seemed to be a less pressurised day. It was a very pleasant task to be able to take those patients well enough and who wished to attend to a short service in the

"NURSE!"
"Yes, Sister?"

hospital chapel mid-morning. The afternoon saw the excited faces of visitors and patients at the start of visiting hours and the less cheery look on departure. The evening wound down with the hospital chaplain standing in the centre of the ward and offering up a prayer or two and ending with a quiet mumbling by all of the "Our Father". The ward would be very still and I'm sure all were conscious of our fleeting mortality.

Matron or her deputy did a ward round mid-morning and late afternoon each day. Sister, if she was on duty, quickly rolled down her sleeves and donned her cuffs. She was usually to be found working in the ward and rarely in the office; so accompanied by Sister, Matron did her round, greeting all the patients, knowing many by name. On occasion a student nurse would be delegated the task of conducting Matron around, and she would expect the student to have every patient's name, diagnosis and care at her fingertips. She would very often divert into the sluice room and bathroom area for an inspection, the outcomes of which were given to Sister.

Visiting time was never a time of idleness. Every evening and Sunday afternoons, drums for sterilising were packed with towels and swabs and made ready for collection. Large amounts of tow curls were made and stored in huge jars, a constant supply always being needed. Medicine bottles were checked for stock and state of the labelling. These were kept in orderly rows in a scrubbed cupboard. This was a great opportunity, too, for the senior to put us through tests to see if we knew the maximum and minimum dosages, the source and usual signs of over-dosage of the commonly used medicines. This knowledge was expected of us and we had to perform.

At the end of visiting with the ringing of a hand bell the relatives left in a very orderly fashion. Many a word of thanks were expressed, rarely a concerned relative would

"NURSE!"
"Yes, Sister?"

ask for a word with Sister. For patients who were critically ill, a special visiting card was issued which allowed for more or less free access. For extra privacy these patients were nursed behind screens. On the issue of a "special" card, in agreement with patients and relatives it was usual to call a minister of religion. This situation would always cast a gloom over the other patients, noticeable by the missing jokes and wisecracks.

The knowledge and skills assimilated with the other students increased daily and the weeks sped by. When I first went into the ward with twenty-eight male patients, their heads seemed automatically to turn to see who was entering the swing doors. I was a very self-conscious seventeen and a half-year-old and felt very gawky. Now I was finishing my allocation, much more assured and fully aware that patients in beds had little else to do other than watch the comings and goings of nurses and other staff, and much more able to take comments like, "Here comes Goldilocks!" without blushing furiously.

It was a requirement to have a work schedule filled in by Sister before leaving the ward. It indicated whether the student had been shown specific skills and had practised them and was proficient. Every practical skill was listed and any unusual ones noted; Sister quizzed the students thoroughly. She had been a stern disciplinarian but never unkind. There was never any familiarly with staff, always a very professional relationship. She was a selfless woman whose life revolved around her work. One thing I will always recall about this Sister; food was still in short supply post-war, but Sister on her meagre salary bought small tins of pineapple, and if there was a patient with a sore mouth or just very ill and needed mouth care she would open a tin of pineapple, chop it up, and give it to the patient to move around his mouth. If he was too weak a small piece was held in forceps and gently swabbed around the patient's

"NURSE!"
"Yes, Sister?"

mouth, very refreshing and much nicer than hospital-issue mouth wash. Pure nursing! In the days before leaving the ward a visit had to be made to the next ward or area of allocation. This was to report to Sister and hand over the work schedule which had been vetted by Matron's administrative sisters.

And so I departed from a work area where I had learned much and had become a fairly assured cog in a big machine; an area which left the greatest impression on me, I think. Now I was to go to another unfamiliar site and was to feel insecure all over again, and with many good wishes from staff and patients I left quite misty eyed.

CHAPTER VI

Time Passing

SINCE STARTING THE TRAINING I FELT I HAD BEEN IN the training environment for ever. Every thought, action and response was immersed in nursing, and yet only six months had passed by. There were murmurings about the first big exam to be taken at the end of the first year, the "State Prelim". This was to be preceded by a hospital examination, considered by many to be the harder of the two. Both exams involved written and practical sections. Extra lessons were arranged, many to be taken off duty. We even went to the schoolroom to brush up our practical skills. Off duty was otherwise spent swotting with little other recreation. I was fortunate to get home if I could arrange two days off together, but our small salary did not allow for too many journeys. Passing the exam had a further incentive: we were awarded a bonus of five pounds – what a treat to look forward to! The outcome, though, was that most was spent on the necessary books for our detailed study of medicine, surgery and so on.

Another event happened at the end of the first year; we were issued our proper uniform, a navy and white striped dress covered by a crisp white apron and stiff belt and collar. Our level of training was indicated by a stripe on the left sleeve. It was very smart and neat after the utility heavy twill dresses. Our enthusiasm for our chosen profession was given quite a lift, and we enjoyed the rustle and crispness of our new image.

CHAPTER VII
Nursing the Sick Children

THE WARD WAS BRIGHT, LIGHT AND AIRY, THE FLOOR sparkling, as was the ward kitchen and other annexes. Iron bedsteads were down the right and metal-barred cots down the left side. The children's ages ranged from three to eleven years old. There were extra trained staff on this ward to monitor the children more closely and the work of the students. Sister was tiny with a huge amount of devotion to those in her charge.

Daily bathing of the children was a fun time, but it took quite some time to get used to handling the little wriggling, wet and slippery bodies, looking into and behind the ears and checking them with the nit comb, especially when being newly admitted, trying to get weight measured, as the child teetered on the scales; trying to avoid a sudden descent on to the hard terrazzo floor and the subsequent injury. The bathroom never, ever being overly warm, preventing chilling was always a factor. I often felt I had been put through a mangle after these sessions.

Oral medicines were not cleverly disguised with flavourings, and encouraging the youngsters to take them required much patience, although we did on occasion resort to a spoonful of jam. The giving of injections was a painful procedure and sorely felt too by the nurses doing the deed. What agony to hold a child in position for a lumber puncture. Thankfully children have short memories of the initial trauma, and at the time long-term effects weren't deeply considered.

"NURSE!"
"Yes, Sister?"

It was not all tears, however; we had jolly times playing games, modelling plasticine, doing puzzles and reading favourite stories, and often just a quiet cuddle. This relaxed time usually occurred in the pre-lunch period. One hilarious moment was when my closest friend, befriended whilst in preliminary training school, pushed a high-backed armchair on the shiny floor, it gathered momentum and we all gazed aghast as it hit the fish tank, scattering glass and goldfish. Screams of delight came from the children as the nurses slid and scrambled around to catch the flopping fish. Sister and the ward domestic were less than pleased to see what had happened to the floor. The rescued fish were put into a large jug as temporary housing, and very soon a globe fish bowl was acquired, to be placed on the central ward cupboard called the stack, a much greater place of safety. This happening was a deciding factor for my friend, who was very upset, to discontinue her training. She had been labouring with more difficulties than the rest of us; she had a very severe limp as a result of poliomyelitis when she was a child, and all the physical stresses and strains had got too much. So although this had been a somewhat amusing episode, the effects were long lasting.

A very sad time of day was the departure of Mummy and Daddy from the bedside at the end of visiting. It was difficult to get around to all the weeping, screaming children to cuddle and pacify them. Sister did keep a sweet jar of jelly babies, but there were no Telly Tubbies or the like to distract these mites, and many sobbed themselves to sleep.

Physically the work was not hard. The consultant paediatrician took great pains in explaining the children's conditions to us, and this was very useful from the point of view of study to come later. It was always stressed not to look upon the youngsters as mini-adults; they suffered different diseases generally to those of adults and needed different treatment and care.

"NURSE!"
"Yes, Sister?"

I do recall a little golden-haired girl of around three years of age, newly admitted. She was extremely ill with miliary tuberculosis, the consultant outlined the condition referring to her chest x-rays. She was started on the new miracle drug Streptomycin. She bloomed initially, the listless little girl showing a little sparkle. Then one morning I came on duty the little one (I still remember her name) was curled up in her cot. From then on she deteriorated, the disease had flared up again. She died.

Being discharged and going home was a day of great pleasure for child, family and staff alike, waves to all at the door, clutching Mummy's hand and a clinic card with a follow-up appointment. Very often on return to the clinic a visit to the ward was made to show us how well they were doing.

Stringent cleaning of the bed/cot was done on discharge of the child. Pillows and sometimes mattresses were sent off for auto-claving. Beds were then made up with pristine linen, all ready for the next unfortunate. It was a light, fun period of nursing practise with its sad moments.

I feel my comments on the linen in this and other circumstances are very necessary. It was always crisp, white and well folded, delivered to each area after lunch in a huge basket. During one study day we were taken on a visit to the hospital laundry. What an amazing sight the fully-functioning work place was. It all looked like very hard work; hot, steamy and very noisy. Firstly the items were sorted, the least pleasant of the jobs. Then sorted linen went into vast vats for washing and boiling. There were small presses, large presses and rollers, the women working in tandem either side of the heated rollers fed the sheets into them dextrously, looped along and folded at the end smelling fresh and feeling warm. The women all wore green wrap around overalls and a turban on their heads; typical East-End ladies, and full of chit-chat over the din

"NURSE!"
"Yes, Sister?"

and making the best of a very hard job. The system, to my unknowing eye, seemed faultless, from the checking in of the vast quantity of used linen to the end packaging of the huge baskets ready for delivery to each site. Fat, fluffy terry towelling baby nappies went through the system by the hundred from the two children's wards and the maternity department and came back like snowflakes. What a pity the persons with the least glamorous jobs got the least reward. It made us all appreciate more our usage of our supplies and suppliers.

CHAPTER VIII
Nursing Patients with Pulmonary Tuberculosis

FROM THE VERY FIRST DAYS OF TRAINING WE, THE students, had been monitored for our susceptibility to tuberculosis. Those who had a positive Heaf or Mantoux test were given a chest x-ray and a thorough medical check-up; for the positive reaction to the tests indicated a previous exposure to the disease and consequent antibody production or indeed the active disease. Those who were negative to the tests indicated no previous exposure to the disease and therefore no acquired immunity, so in this instance the student was vaccinated with the BCG vaccine and this created immunity. pulmonary tuberculosis was very active in the community in the post-war years due to social deprivation.

Mid-training the allocation list indicated that I was for night duty on the ward with male patients suffering from pulmonary tuberculosis, twenty-eight patients in the ward and six outside on a veranda, the latter being the most actively diseased. The shift was eight p.m. to eight a.m.

It was not a very heavy nursing allocation but a very lonely one. One relatively junior nurse overseeing so many patients would not be acceptable today. The duties were straight forward, starting with the giving out of a warm night drink of cocoa or Ovaltine. There were many pairs of willing hands to help with this task, many of the patients frustrated by the enforced inactivity of the long days, physical rest being the mainstay of their treatment. Only a few patients required an early morning and evening

> "NURSE!"
> "Yes, Sister?"

recording of TPR. Rarely there was a patient who was very ill, and needed all the basic care for the terminally ill, and if this was the case another nurse was sent to work with me to make the patient comfortable for the night. Medications were given when Night Sister did her early round, but mostly it was linctus to suppress coughs. Masks and gowns were worn when caring for the patients on the veranda. The rationale for the care in such an airy environment was commonplace, as it had been for many years for the rich with consumption to travel to Switzerland, for example, to take the air and get cured.

Gradually the ambulant patients went into their beds, and after tucking in and adjusting bedding and pillows it was lights out. There were many occasions when a yelp was heard as a long-legged youth stretched himself out, only to find he was in an apple-pie bed; but mostly it was the young men who played tricks on the older, and from this often stemmed hilarity which led to pillows being thrown and biffed. It was not always easy for a five-foot-nothing eighteen-year-old to call them to order.

Because of the risk of infection the nurse on duty remained in the office, outside of the ward which had a viewing window. The ward, as were all, was of the Nightingale type, with the usual facilities at either end. The office was small and contained a built-in linen cupboard and a tiny type of larder cupboard, in which the precious tea ration and other not very available items like sugar and stout were stored. Also in the office was a chair and desk. The flooring was of a dark green, heavy, rubberised lino, highly polished with not a speck of dust. Not an item was present to relieve the austerity of the scene.

Using a torch a ward round was done every half hour. At midnight a document entitled the "Midnight Return" had to be filled in; this required the details of the number of patients who were present, had been discharged, newly

"NURSE!"
"Yes, Sister?"

admitted or had died. These documents were collected soon after by a member of the nursing team based in the "Night Office".

It was a very lonely allocation, with plenty of time for reading. One of the least amusing things to occur whilst sitting quietly was to hear the slightest of sounds, a slight scratching; it was the sound of huge cockroaches, possibly stag beetles marching across the green lino floor. It was a relief to enter the ward to hear the snores, grunts and other sounds emitted from slumbering humankind.

The night hours seemed long initially. The night office was always available by telephone if there was a need. After the "meal relief" came along around midnight and after a chat with colleagues at the same meal break, each exchanging our allocation experiences, the night soon sped by. Then a round was done by Sister around two a.m. On a number of occasions I went to the entrance to peer down the long, long corridor, only to see a nurse's apron or doctor's white coat flapping in the eerie distance, hastening to their necessary care.

A task for the wee small hours was the slicing and buttering of bread ready for breakfast, laid on a moist towel and covered likewise. Some of the slices were appalling, but I soon learned to be more skilful. The margarine had to be used very sparingly as each ward had a set ration.

The night report was written at around four to five a.m.; and wake-up call came around six a.m. Usually one or two of the patients would get up and give the other patients an early morning cup of tea, invariably these were the older patients with a well-ingrained work ethic. In the meantime I sped around to take the necessary readings of temperatures, hoping the tea had not been sipped before I got there. After this the early morning medications had to be given, for this a senior nurse came to check and assist. Now with all the patients stirring, bowls of hot water were

"NURSE!"
"Yes, Sister?"

given to those confined to bed for a freshen-up wash; later in the day they'd have a full wash down. Those up and about patiently awaited the chance to get to the bathroom, which housed the two small wash basins! For those unable, a wash was given, and pillows and sheets made comfortable. Quite often able patients would shave someone else in need, with a great deal of chit-chat.

Night Sister did her rounds in all this hustle and bustle. She greeted every patient and spent time speaking to those very sick, many of whom were war veterans. The rest of the morning was spent making up beds and putting out breakfast trays, ready for the meal to arrive around seven thirty a.m. With the refreshed day staff coming on duty, breakfast was soon served. Finally the night report was read to the nurse in charge, rather a daunting task initially, and then I had to conduct the nurse around the ward to each patient and point out any changes or observations, confirming the content of the night report.

A wave from the ward door, always acknowledged by the patients, and off to a meal and bed. I was very fortunate that I slept soundly all day until called at six p.m. The allocation was for three months' duration, with five nights on duty and two off per week.

CHAPTER IX
Operating Theatre

MY ALLOCATION TO THE OPERATING THEATRE CAME latterly in my second year. I had some idea of the atmosphere in the operating theatre, having escorted patients from the surgical ward; it was usual if there were enough staff on the ward to stay and watch the operation being performed, and this I had done a few times. On these occasions I was full of fear and scared of touching something sterile or impeding the work. Masked and gowned figures silently went about their business. Fortunately the theatre porters were very knowledgeable and seemed very much part of the team and soon put me on the right path in the outer areas of the theatre. Escorting the patient for surgery was as worrying for the inexperienced nurse as for the patient. Squeezing the patient's hand was as much for my benefit as for the patient, though one had to put on the face and voice of bravery.

This area, then, was to be my new allocation. The student nurses on duty at one time would be three or four, with a like number of trained staff always monitoring the learners. There was much to learn in this totally different environment when it came to equipment – from steam belching from water sterilisers, like huge pressure cookers, to sets and sets of surgical instruments plunged into vast tanks of boiling water on perforated trays for sterilising – and our various duties before, during and after surgery – capping, gowning and gloving, finding it extremely difficult to reach up and tie the top tapes for a very tall surgeon, and

"NURSE!"
"Yes, Sister?"

the crucial job of correctly positioning the patient on the table, with the staff always trying to maintain the patient's dignity and modesty and respect for the patient now unconscious and totally in our hands.

Being ever watchful whilst the operation was in progress, generally there was only muted conversation and instruction from behind the masks and an occasional clatter of metal against metal. Checking and re-checking swabs and instrumentation numbers with the nurse at the table and correlating them with those on the indicator board, fetching supplies, adjusting and repositioning lights, stands and other machinery: all this whilst wearing unaccustomed clothing and boots. Certainly it was hard and tiring initially, but how much more so for the surgeons, anaesthetists and all working and standing for hours on end at the table.

The working day started with the washing down of all theatre walls and all exposed surfaces. The anaesthetic room was checked by trained nurses. The gas machine and suction equipment were tested for correct functioning. Meanwhile the sterilising room team prepared towel-draped trolleys with sets of instruments; all were masked and gowned with minimum chattering.

The operating lists, having been drawn up by Surgeon and Sister the day before, were worked through; very often the surgeons, anaesthetists and nurses at the table didn't get a break for hours. Inevitably the lists were sometimes delayed by an emergency that had to be dealt with immediately in the main theatre; and if that was the case the secondary theatre, really just a tiled room with a table, lighting and minimal equipment, was brought into action to continue the lists, as I recall with a well thought out plan of procedure, and not simply improvisation.

At the completion of the lists there was much to do in readiness for the next day's work: cleaning, sorting, packing up instruments; and with the constant handling it did not

"NURSE!"
"Yes, Sister?"

take too long to learn the names and functions. Soon all was ready for the re-sterilising. Packing linen, towel drapes, and dressings in counted bundles, these had to be counted and recounted before tying with thread; all this type of material was packed into drums with vents on the side, and when complete, off to the autoclave. The other half of the nursing team were washing down walls, floors and all the standing equipment and overhead lighting. The atmosphere was always good humoured as we plodded on; no time for boredom. It all drove home to us the need for scrupulous cleanliness at all times and in all areas. This work continued until all was finished, however late the hour.

Surgery over the weekends was minimal and of an emergency nature only, so the staff spent their time checking all the stocks and restocking and reordering. It was a time for giggles and girlie talk too, opportunities for which in our training was a rarity, especially in a ward environment, which was ordered and orderly, with numerous protocols which had been tried and tested over many decades as a consequence of the influence of Florence Nightingale and the military systems.

So we stood tittering and jibing as we tested the many hundreds of surgeon's gloves for soundness, which were used and reused many times, powdered and packed in linen folders ready for sterilising. It was a time too when the trained staff had an opportunity to demonstrate items of equipment: suckers, operating tables and fittings, diathermy machines, giving details of uses and dangers. We trawled through shelves of instruments, learning their names and uses, how various instruments constructed of different materials were sterilised. There was even an Aladdin's cave in Sister's office where she kept stored the scopes, the very costly, delicately engineered equipment, in rich wooden boxes often lined with velvet. These would have been the forerunners of the fibre optic scopes of today. It was only

> *"NURSE!"*
> *"Yes, Sister?"*

the most senior staff or surgeons who were allowed to handle them.

Being allowed to scrub was restricted to the last few weeks of allocation when it was considered we had sufficient understanding and ability. The occasion was usually when the surgeon was working solo and in which only instruments were passed – e.g. in gynaecology and ear, nose and throat surgery – and which was of short duration. What excitement, feeling as if one was performing for a major case. A trained member was hovering and ready to step in. The experience was made very interesting in that the surgeon would point out anatomical landmarks and various abnormalities. The hours spent swotting up on bones and anatomical models were made relevant and worthwhile.

Each day was a challenge, not knowing what each individual case would bring up: the delight of a baby's first cry at a Caesarean section brought in as an emergency, the midwifery staff showing undeniable signs of relief. Counter to this was the unexpected death of a patient having what was considered a very minor operation, the devastation was felt by one and all. It was a very technical type of nursing experience, but there was much caring shown to the patients and students and it gave us a greater understanding of the nursing needs of the post-operative patient and of the correct pre-operative preparation of the patient for surgery.

Schedules were filled in at the end of allocation by sisters and staff nurses who had vetted our work. As one set of learners left, so another filled our shoes. What a wonderful team worked in theatres; they had shown infinite patience and now had to take on more learners, all agog but unversed in the special intricacies of theatre work.

CHAPTER X
Female Surgical Nursing

OUR TRAINING DAYS WERE PROGRESSING WELL. THOSE feeling homesick were happier as the days passed and they could think of holidays. Experiences were shared sitting on beds and floors in our little rooms and I was the oddball being English but wasn't deterred, and we got on well. The exchange of views and situations we had met was invaluable in preparation for our next allocation.

The surgical ward was quite a different environment from that of the adult medical ward. The patients' needs had changed emphasis, and were very often of an urgent nature. The previously taught and stressed phrase "know and observe your patient" was at least, if not more, important in this setting, as a surgical scene can alter in seconds.

Sister on this ward was labelled as "one to be feared". On reporting to the ward initially she was brusque and had no time for chat. The staff nurse was an unflappable, quiet, supportive young lady who carried on regardless of the difficulties. Both in their own way were super nurses, I later learnt.

The ward was situated on the top floor of a three storey building and therefore got maximum light. The wooden floors glistened and in the late afternoon sunbeams streamed in across the ward to dazzle patients and nurses; so very different to the foggy days spent in the medical ward. The ward was always immaculate, however active. Sister had a reputation for minimising the numbers of wheelchairs

"NURSE!"
"Yes, Sister?"

and trolleys entering her ward and leaving tyre tracks on her glossy floor. To be honest, when Sister was off duty the atmosphere became a little more relaxed.

One Saturday afternoon, there were few patients in this twenty-eight-bed ward; a colleague from my class from preliminary training school was working alongside me and we were making up clean beds. We started singing the favourite tunes of the day, the patients joined in too. The best-known tune and the most lustily sung was "Too Young" (made popular by the ever present Jimmy Young of radio fame). It was a pleasant interlude in what was a busy and tense allocation. We were very grateful to Staff Nurse and tried not to let the cat out of the bag or let her down.

One Sunday, by way of comparison, Sister was on duty.
"Nurse!"
"Yes, Sister?"

She was standing beside a wheelchair by her office. In the chair was a wizened little lady of about sixty years of age, very old to someone just turned eighteen. She was wearing a sweaty turban and looked thin and work weary. Many women wore such head gear during and after the war whilst working in factories.

"Bring the patient to the bathroom and then put on a cap and gown," were my instructions. "I'll be with you in a few minutes."

I seated the patient on a chair in the confined space of the bathroom and found out by chatting with her she lived and worked nearby. Sister came in. "Remove the turban," she directed. This I did with some caution. It was matted to the hair and a large swelling on the back of the head into the nape of her neck. Sister peered and I looked. It was a large tumour the shape of a doughnut. The stench was awful. It had not been uncovered for weeks.

The poor soul said, "I didn't know what to do, it has been growing for weeks."

"NURSE!"
"Yes, Sister?"

"Cut the hair and cleanse the tumour, put on a light dressing and triangular bandage as a turban."

Exit Sister, the bathroom door closed. Offering a few words of comfort to the distressed lady I busied myself collecting the tools of my trade. As I worked, not knowing the possible outcome of her treatment, we talked. What a hard-working lady she was, and still very eager to get back to home and family. Before we left the bathroom she had an admission bath with plenty of hot water but no pretty-smelling soap or bubbles, just a piece of carbolic block soap that was ward issue and a square of recycled towelling from the linen room as a flannel. She was more than thankful for her care, and so wrapped up in hospital-issue nightie and dressing gown, I tucked her into her bed and reported to Sister the completion of the task, then went off to clear the bathroom. It was another learning experience.

On this allocation many practical skills had to be perfected. Passing a not so fine red rubber tube with a lead-weighted end through a nostril and down into a stomach, for washing out or feeding purposes on a real live patient, was quite a different challenge from classroom practise on a manikin. Many convincing explanations were needed, and many patients were mystified by questions about broken noses. Firstly I had to watch a senior nurse perform this skill and then when the opportunity arose I was monitored carrying out the task, and after being observed on a number of occasions was classed as competent. This was never a happy situation for the patient, especially when I had to explain I was a novice and had to be supervised. The expression, "You have to learn on someone; it might as well be me," was often used by the always-understanding East-Ender.

Escorting the patients to the operating theatre was almost a daily occurrence. A ritual was followed in each instance in getting the patient ready in respect to basic care;

"NURSE!"
"Yes, Sister?"

variations occurred for specific operations and in those circumstances preparations might start days before surgery. For planned surgery it was usually a junior's task to shave and bath the patient, this on the male patients this task was performed by the hospital barber. After the bath an open-backed gown was donned, thick woolly socks and theatre cap on the head.

The patient was fasting from the night before usually, but if the patient was on a list late she might be given tea and toast. If there was a delay this could cause much distress, but it was always important to err on the side of caution. The time in preparation was precious from the point of view of reassurances and answering the many questions asked; we were in the days when patients were uninformed: TV hospital soaps were yet to come. The patients were very trusting. Finally the patient emptied her bladder and the urine was tested, the results being vital for the anaesthetist. The surgeon too did not want a full bladder getting in the way of the knife.

Pre-medication was the final task, with the cleanly to bed patient lying on her canvas stretcher sheet. A trained member of staff would be in attendance for the issue, checking and observation of the administration of the drug. The drug was controlled by the Dangerous Drugs Act. The drugs at this time before the advent of glass ampoules were in the form of minute tablets, which had to be dissolved in water. A teaspoon was used and a few minims of water were boiled over a tiny glass Bunsen burner and the tablet dissolved in it, the solution was then drawn up into a syringe. Together with the trained nurse the student went to the bedside with the patient's case notes; after checking the patient name and details verbally with the patient and the documents, the drug was given and duly signed for as done. A further important task before leaving the drug cupboard was the checking of the stock remaining against

"NURSE!"
"Yes, Sister?"

the drug register. This ritual, though time consuming, was essential for all concerned in the handling of dangerous drugs.

So now the patient was sedated and lying waiting; a fearful time for most people. Walking alongside the patient on the trolley, along corridors and into lifts, with them just seeing the ceiling lights speed by in a sedated haze. It was good that the patient could see your familiar face at her side and touch a reassuring hand.

Mostly patients returned from surgery unconscious with a rubber airway in place. The journey back to the ward could be a worrying few minutes, even though emergency instruments were available. It was a relief to reach the bedside with the waiting staff and other resuscitation equipment. As soon as the patient started to recover from the anaesthetic she was gradually raised up, from two to four pillows. Vomiting was often a problem with the type of anaesthetic used in those days, a source of great distress, especially if the patient had abdominal stitches.

One of the tools of the trade, in the surgical environment especially, was a "donkey". This comprised of a firm pillow tightly rolled into a twill draw sheet. The log was placed under the patient's knees and the sheet tails tucked tightly under the mattress; the theory according to the knowledge of the day was that it prevented the patient slipping down the bed. This it did to a degree, helping breathing and the drainage of fluid. Side-effects of its use in the form of thrombosis eventually precluded its use. However, it was quite a few years more before "early ambulation" became the norm. Keeping the patients confined to bed for weeks on end was quite usual, and the nursing needs therefore very extensive.

Wound dressings were usually changed daily, especially if a drain was used. No preparations for these surgical procedures were started until all sweeping, dusting and bed

"NURSE!"
"Yes, Sister?"

making had been completed for one hour. The ward steriliser, a large, chromed-steel square tank, was filled with water and boiled. Bowls, kidney dishes and instruments all went in. It was sited midway down the ward with the sink alongside. This was the hive of activity. The dressing trolleys were washed down and draped with sterile towels and with much dexterity, using Cheatles forceps, the sterilised bowls, instruments and so on, were laid out and covered with a further towel. This was the task of the designated senior nurse. My role at this stage of my training was to screen the bed, position the patient, pour the lotions, and on completion of the dressing by the senior to fix the dressing with zinc oxide tape, which may have been further supported by a many-tail or T bandage. I watched closely the dressing technique, which often included clips and stitch removal or drain shortening, and eagerly awaited my chance to act as dresser.

It became very evident how important grooming of hair, hands and nails were for us; hands and nails were constantly being scrubbed, forever the short nails, never to grow long or wear polish, hair back under the cap and business-like standards never to be let slip. The patients were very vulnerable to infection and at our mercy. Face masks were always worn and speech was kept to a minimum during any aseptic technique. Some senior nurses would relate our practise to our theoretical knowledge and spend time on quizzing us on bacteriology and the spread of infection, especially in the minutes to spare when the ward was quiet with visitors.

Using blood transfusions during and post-surgery was fairly common. The equipment used was sterilised in a metal tin and was comprised of glass tubes and drip chamber, red rubber bung, rubber tubing and metal control clips. The blood was issued in glass bottles, a full pint of blood and giving set were supplied by the National Blood

"NURSE!"
"Yes, Sister?"

Transfusion Service. The checking of group names, numbers, and so on on labels was rigorous, all being verified with patients' case notes and with laboratory and trained staff. The students' tasks whilst the transfusion was in progress were to monitor the patient's pulse, respiration and skin colour for rashes and her general demeanour, initially every fifteen minutes for an hour and then every hour, hopefully to detect quickly any adverse reaction. From the pallor of anaemia the patient passed often to having a rosy glow.

Later surgical allocations involved orthopaedic surgery on a female ward. This mainly involved fractured limbs needing a surgical repair, but many were cases of fractured hips in aged ladies. The treatment usually involved putting the leg in full extension using a steel pin through the bone at the end of the femur, and this then was attached to cords and weights, held in a splint on a pulley system. Often being aged the tissues were slow to heal, and the effects of almost total immobilisation for weeks on end had a devastating effect on lungs and pressure areas. It was a very heavy and distressing nursing scene, each patient needing total bed nursing care with much mental encouragement, many of them becoming confused and demented during the weeks in bed.

Advances in surgery were, however, taking place, and I was fortunate to be on duty when the first patient in our hospital came back from surgery with a "new hip". The patient was up and about within the first forty-eight hours, sitting in her chair and taking her first tottering steps with the physiotherapists' clapping and cheering accompanying her efforts. What a wonderful day it was. Yes, it was an exciting allocation.

CHAPTER XI
Social Life during Training

OFF DUTY WAS GENERALLY A MIX OF CHATTING AND studying together, especially in the early months. As said previously, there was little money in our pockets and by the time essentials like stockings and a pretty-smelling tablet of soap were bought we were often penniless. The Irish girls also tried to save from their pittance their fare home for a once-yearly visit. However, we were not miserable. Life for all was pretty austere. The age of spend, spend, spend was not yet with us, and our rewards were in our chosen work.

Once organised, we had plenty to occupy our time with the Student Nurses Association, an arm of the Royal College of Nursing. During our second year it became very active; calling elections for chair persons and secretary, the formalities of meetings being a new field to all of us. It was through this medium we brought the students' point of view to the hierarchy and a few changes were made, mostly to do with the living in-house situation. After a few flops we organised some successful dances. We invited local college students and had a good time, being overseen by Home Sister and other seniors. In those days eighteen to twenty-year-old ladies were not very male-orientated from the social point of view, and all in all these dances were very decorous affairs. The nurses' home was called "The Nunnery". It was not until the third year of training that the wings started to be spread, spending our days off simply shop window gazing on Oxford Street and then being very

"NURSE!"
"Yes, Sister?"

extravagant by going into Lyon's Corner House for tea and cake. Later, developing a little more "street cred", the buzz was to go dancing, the Hammersmith and Victoria Palais' being the most popular and accessible haunts. We were kindly treated by some entertainment houses with free tickets for shows and the cinema. After all these outings we had to be back in the hospital before a certain time, and the head porter at the entrance knew us all by name and chided us for running over our time, but never more than that.

Matron held delightful events. In the summer it was a strawberry and cream tea garden party. All the medical and nursing staff attended, and a few hospital management committee members. How Matron managed it I do not know, but the sun always shone on her efforts. This was very much a luxury event in this still post-war era.

Christmas brought us a staff dinner with all the trimmings. It was a wonderful spread, but with so many to cater for a number were held over the weeks following Christmas day. It was a thank you gesture from the hospital management committee of the day and was followed by Matron's "Staff Dance", which was a very formal affair. It seemed another world from starched aprons to evening gowns for the lucky few, but we all did our best to "pretty up".

Christmas also saw the staff concert, organised by a senior pharmacist. Year after year, the hidden talents of everyone certainly came to the fore. For those inveigled into participating, the rehearsals were exciting and at times very fraught. The nights of the big shows, usually two, went as all amateur shows go; hitches galore, curtains snagging, tuneless singing, scenery collapsing, acts over-running and participants absent. They were times of great enjoyment, with patients and staff alike full of appreciation; and on reflection they were amazingly successful.

Some of the most poignantly felt memories of Christmas

"NURSE!"
"Yes, Sister?"

were of nurses, doctors and other staff gathering on Christmas Eve at the front entrance of the main corridor. We, the nurses, wore our cloaks with the red lining on the outside; we each carried a lantern with a candle or a torch. The hospital chaplains led the column of carol singers – nurses, doctors and other staff – up and down stairs, along darkened corridors, into, through and over connecting bridges, lights twinkling. Into and around every ward we went. Many a patient's face shone with tears, moved and lonesome for their own families. The sight and sound was haunting, the echoes travelled along the empty corridors for many minutes. When we had traversed all areas it was usually just before midnight, so after a quick cup of tea and a biscuit, off we went to midnight services in the hospital chapel or local churches. It was a long night!

In keeping with tradition, a great day of celebration came once a year. Prize-giving day was held on 30 November, St Andrew's Day. We were all very conscious of our good traditions and tried to uphold them. Awards were made in relation to marks achieved in examinations, covering all aspects of our studies and nursing skills. Nursing administration staff and ward sisters gathered to discuss nominees and select award winners. The big day was also, for those who had been successful in the Final Hospital Examination, a time to receive the coveted hospital badge and certificate. A local dignitary or celebrity usually did the honours, and this was followed by a buffet tea and in the evening a dance. Local press were present to take the details and photograph the scene. On looking back, it would be difficult to find a more beautiful, fresh-faced group of young ladies, immaculate in their sparkling uniforms.

CHAPTER XII
Classroom Days

OUR FORMAL THEORETICAL AND PRACTICAL TRAINING commenced in the preliminary training school and following this took place on study days. This made things very hard on the wards as it meant staffing levels were reduced. This really did not become very apparent until the mid-years of training when there was a noticeable drop in numbers starting training; no classes of thirty again.

We were taught theory and practice of nursing and the patients' needs in specialities, a phase further on from the basics of preliminary training and related to our ward allocation. Physicians and surgeons, pathologists and bacteriologists and all other field experts expounded on the clinical conditions of the patients we were nursing. Practical nursing care teaching covered the more advanced techniques needed in these domains. We stood in awe whilst Sister Tutor explained the function of Southey's tubes, which were tiny, silver cannulae inserted into waterlogged tissues of the lower limbs to drain them or explain what seemed to be the barbaric technique of scarification for the same circumstances. Some of the methods were ingenious, and now drugs do it all.

Later educational methods changed and a "Block System" of schooling took over. Students were in the classroom for a week or two, depending on the topics to be covered and the stage of training. Overall this was beneficial as the student got a mind-set for a longer period and the wards knew the students were not available. It was becoming apparent that

"NURSE!"
"Yes, Sister?"

the National Health Service was having difficulty in maintaining staff levels.

At the end of the first year a State Preliminary Examination had to be taken; a written examination covering anatomy and physiology, hygiene, first aid, and dietetics. This was followed by a practical skills examination, which also involved questioning. These examinations had to be passed before going on in training. State Final Papers at the end of the three years were over a full day, followed a week later by a gruelling "practical" session. In this, nursing situations were created and candidates had to plan and proceed as if working in a ward situation. The scene was set and monitored by a "State Examiner", who was a very experienced matron or sister tutor, specifically appointed by the nurses' controlling body, The General Nursing Council.

The whole situation could not have taken place without the cooperation and indomitable spirit of a selected number of our cockney patients. Patients from the wards, if in fair health and almost ready for discharge, were brought to the examination room. These good souls volunteered, after full explanation was given to them of their role. It was amusing to get a whisper out of the corner of the patient's mouth if he/she had spotted an error or that we had forgotten to do this or that. As these examinations went on for a few days, we needed a group of role-players and we were never short of these kind-hearted people.

Six weeks later the results were delivered in the early post; so a gaggle of finalists and prelim candidates gathered around Matron's office. It was generally known that if you had a thin envelope then you had passed, but if you had a fatter one it contained re-sit forms, therefore a failure. There were many trembling hands, tears and laughter outside Matron's office on that morning, but for myself I had not attained the necessary age of twenty-one years to sit the final examination, so I had to await a further full year.

"NURSE!"
"Yes, Sister?"

This was not a bad thing. I had started training knowing this and I had a full year to gain further theory and develop more practically.

The big day came, however, with success. Off we all trooped to the needle room where the ever patient and kindly needle woman measured us for our navy blue belts, a prized and outward sign when worn, of being a State Registered Nurse, soon to be followed by the distinctive badge. A few days later we collected our belts from the needle room and preened in the mirror, possibly with the delight of the moment, not being fully alert to the responsibilities now carried. But this is what we had studied and worked hard for, and so we took on our new role of Staff Nurse.

CHAPTER XIII
Night Duty in the Smog of '52

THE CLIMATE OF LONDON WAS GENERALLY DARK AND gloomy in the winter months, until the "Clean Air Act" of 1956 came into force. This was legislation introduced finally in response to the ever-increasing levels of atmospheric pollution which culminated eventually in the "smog" of 1952, which resulted in numerous lost lives. The fog that descended over London in December 1952 was laden with noxious products from countless industrial and domestic chimneys. Being on the river, damp mist percolated into every nook and cranny and not a whisper of a breeze was present to move it onwards. It was to persist for a good four days, so whilst I slept, which I never found difficult on night duty, the yellow-green haze descended.

Walking from the dining room out ino the main corridor, which extended from the front entrance to the doors of the maternity unit, a distance often considered by us to be half a mile as we trudged it, we saw the distant doors and signposts were obscured. Mention had been made of it being a foggy night whilst we were having our meal before duty, but we were quite unprepared for what we saw. The air left a sting in the nostrils and a bitter taste in the mouth and made the eyes water. The yellow fog swirled along the high ceilings as we, a subdued group, split to go to our separate wards of allocation. We had not seen anything like this before. I was working on a medical ward.

During the day every empty bed had been filled with patients in acute respiratory distress. There were contingency

"NURSE!"
"Yes, Sister?"

plans to bring in two extra beds to each ward if the need arose, or indeed just to use mattresses on the floor. All the surgical beds also had been taken over. Day staff were very supportive, they had had a very hectic shift and were much delayed going off duty. There was a great tension felt by all the doctors and nurses. It was really an emergency situation that we had to do our best to overcome.

From the ward entrance door to the end of the ward the fog moved silently around the central lights. Now, as I was quite a senior nurse – all of three years' experience with a junior to oversee – my priority was to check the supply of oxygen and make sure all delivery systems were functioning. Porters came with a clatter and bang; however quiet we tried to be, metal keys on metal cylinders are not conducive to rest. Wheeling a cylinder in, taking the empty one out; it was a clatter. No piped oxygen for us.

The oxygen was given via a number of methods; one was a pair of spectacles with tiny capillary rubber tubes which entered the nostrils; the other, a rather heavy-weight affair with a mask to cover nose and mouth with a breathing bag attached, made in heavy green rubber, was called a BLB mask (Boothby, Lovelace and Balblian). We used anything available the need was so great. Every pillow was in use and we needed more; back rests were fully extended and we rolled blankets to form the base of the pillow pile. Whilst the fog remained there was little one could do but keep the patients comfortable and give oxygen.

For the days the fog persisted a number of our patients died, numbered amongst the many thousands in London at the time. Estimates quote ten to fifteen thousand deaths, but the figure will never be truly known. There is much documented evidence of this horrendous week in the life of London.

CHAPTER XIV
Casualty and Out Patients

THE DAY STARTED WITH SCRUBBING AND POLISHING the wound-dressing areas, tables and trolleys, stacking lotions, bandages and splints in readiness for the flow of patients to commence around nine a.m. for casualty dressings and out patients.

This was an allocation taken in the later months of the three-year training. There were three distinct areas to work in; emergency admission, casualty, and out-patients clinics, each requiring different approaches and skills. It was stressed very often that we were now under scrutiny by the public and that dress and behaviour must be beyond reproach.

Trained staff generally worked in the admission area where patients came in off the ambulances. Traffic accidents were not on the scale of today's happenings, and patients were usually very acutely ill with respiratory, cardiac, renal and cerebral conditions, many having suffered long years of neglect of conditions which now had become chronic, the NHS and GP services being a very new phenomenon. The student nurses' duties in relation to the admissions area were generally to chaperone the female patients and to escort the newly-admitted to the wards.

I do recall one sleepy Sunday morning working in admissions. Staffing was light and the medical officer had been called down to an emergency admission. I was helping a trained nurse to strip a young man of strong physique for examination. He was of Scandinavian origin with blonde hair and fine, handsome features. He was a seaman brought

"NURSE!"
"Yes, Sister?"

in from the local docks and had been involved in a fight. His abdomen showed three small punctures. He died on the trolley. I felt unwell and sad for the rest of the day. It was the first time I had come up against the harsh reality of someone deliberately inflicting a wound that would kill.

In the casualty area new patients were seen by the MO then forwarded with the treatment card to the waiting area, then taken in strict rotation and treated. It was some days before I developed a strong enough voice to be heard above the hubbub when calling the patient's name. We had often all had it impressed on us to speak with muted tones and maintain silence.

In the dressing room a huge, enamel-topped table sat, and at each corner a nurse carried out her dressing duties. Stitches needed dressing, stitches needed removal, septic fingers for soaking, patients sitting in corners spoon-bathing a swollen eye. One vital area of care was the careful monitoring of a patient's response to a trial dose of Tetanus Antitoxin (horse serum). This was in case a severe reaction to the serum developed. If the full dose was given it might have resulted in an anaphylactic shock and may have proved fatal. There was much to learn!

The bandaging skills learnt in the heady days of preliminary training school came to the fore with neat application of figure-of-eights to knee and foot and application of slings to the many with arm injuries. The trained staff were plentiful and always vetting one's work and available if advice was needed. The hectic time was the mornings; the patients were very patient as they queued, first for the doctor then for the care and then over to the almoner's office where they had another wait if they had social or monetary problems.

Out-patients clinics were held in the afternoons, the physicians and surgeons being on the wards or in surgery during the morning. Many and varied were the clinics, from

"NURSE!"
"Yes, Sister?"

general medicine and surgery to opthalmics, dermatology and all the specialities. A vast number of patients attended the pulmonary tuberculosis clinic, many patients from the wards often attended for a pneumothorax fill-up. This was the treatment of choice for PTB before the advent of the anti-tubercular drugs. The pneumothorax involved inserting a large needle into the chest in an effort to collapse a section of lung, this collapsed the tubercular cavity and allowed it to rest and heal. It was quite a while before I understood the mechanics of the AP (artificial pneumothorax) machinery with its complex gauges, tubes and pump systems.

Congested corridors were the norm with wheelchairs and crutches often impeding the walkers. Seeking case notes, seeking x-rays and pathology reports, trying to placate one and all 'til the last poor soul was left and peace descended.

The opportunities for learning were numerous and if the consultant was not under too much pressure he would spend minutes explaining details of the patients' signs and symptoms. He would, however, expect you to know the relevant anatomy and physiology. The patients were quiet and gracious, uncomplaining always, most grateful for any attention given. There were no padded seats in a warm, airy environment, just ancient wooden benches possibly dating from the sick asylum days of 1868, in a gloomy, stone-floored atrium and corridors. In the winter month's damp, sodden overcoats and shoes gave off a quite distinctive odour.

With an extra twelve months of training to complete I did have some weeks spent on night duty, admissions and casualty. Most of the time I was alone and when more than one person was to be admitted an extra nurse was sent down to assist. Weekends could be lively with the pubs emptying and the resulting punch-ups. Stitches in wounds

"NURSE!"
"Yes, Sister?"

meant the callout of the casualty officer on duty; the Metropolitan Police were a great asset in attending and controlling lively situations; the adjacent porter's lodge meant that porters too were available and rendered valuable assistance.

Vital to the running of the hospital were the figures furnished by the wards on their "Midnight Returns"; one of my tasks just after midnight was to collect the documents and to collate these figures, which showed for each ward the numbers of patients, those discharged, admitted and those deceased. The details always included new patients' religions, and it was not an unusual occurrence to meet a cleric in the silent corridors as we both went to our separate duties in the dead of night.

In the busy early morning hours of work on the wards, when the admission department was silent, Night Sister in charge, knowing the circumstances in each ward, would direct me to work where the need was greatest; to be called back to the department if a casualty arrived or an admission was expected. It was an interesting allocation that highlighted the creaks, groans and smells of an old building at night as I walked the corridors and wards. Housing much human heartache and endeavour throughout the long night hours, always with the new admissions and constant trickle of casualties, a hospital never ceases to function.

CHAPTER XV

Nursing the Sick Babies

NOT AN AREA I WAS LOOKING FORWARD TO, HAVING no experience with infants in my life, but the fact of having worked with three-year-olds earlier in my training was a help.

This allocation was for "the babies' ward", ages ranging from a few weeks of age to three years. The ward was situated on the top floor, light and bright with magnolia glossed walls. Murals had not become a feature of hospitals at that time. The sides of the ward were lined with metal drop-sided cots and at front leading into the ward were two glass cubicles on either side. One was Sister's office, the other housed one, two and three cots, and in these were nursed the very acutely ill babies, closely overseen by Sister.

The kitchen with its terrazzo floor, huge wooden dresser and deep sink, had as its centrepiece a large, well-scrubbed table. Large heavy kettles were kept boiling on a gas cooker. It was in this environment we masked and gowned, to make, under close supervision, the babies' bottle feeds. The bottles and teats were sterilised in large enamel tanks of hypochlorite solution. Depending on the number of bottle-fed babies on the ward, the working through the compiled list may have taken many hours; with the patient measuring of the powder and mixing with boiled water, filling and capping the bottles, sufficient having to be prepared for the twenty-four hours and stacked carefully in the refrigerator.

Now competent to make up a baby's feed, it was time to be shown how to feed a baby! Masked and gowned, hands washed and trembling, having watched a senior demonstrate,

"NURSE!"
"Yes, Sister?"

now it was my turn. Seated on a low nursing chair, terrified of choking an already sick infant, another hurdle was taken; feeding a baby with cleft palate and a hare lip was a worrying time. We were not left alone until we were quite able and self-assured.

Learning how to take routine observations of a small infant was quite a different thing to the ease developed with adults. A child squirming around was not an easy subject to monitor, and not being able to explain to the babe was quite stressful. Likewise the hesitant handling of a soapy, slippery baby at bath time made me hold my breath until assurance took over, but all these obstacles were overcome after observed practise.

Generally the admissions to the ward were straightforward chest infections and once apyrexial and hydrated the babies passed from being almost moribund to within hours cooing and gurgling. So too with the mite admitted profoundly dehydrated with pyloric stenosis, after the test feed produced a projectile vomit it was off to the theatre stat on a cruciform splint, returning safely after a simple operation and as soon was wide awake, guzzling liquid from a bottle and teat. Almost miraculous.

It being winter in foggy London one Saturday afternoon we admitted in quick succession two very young infants with bronchiolitis. In those days a metal and perspex box was used (Charlotte's Box) which fitted totally over the babe and oxygen was fed into it and was used to provide a well-oxygenated atmosphere.

We had one in use and had to run to the adjacent maternity unit for the loan of another. Within a short space of time two more mites were admitted acutely ill. The parents handed them over, trusting, and so very often had to rush home to look after the rest of the family. It was an horrendous afternoon, and not all of our ministrations were successful. It was a delight, however, to see the many go home well and loved, it was sad to think that due to the poor living conditions many would return.

COMPLETION

It was July 1953 and I had at last reached twenty-one years of age; in fact it did turn out to be special as an educational innovation was introduced, and on my actual birthday a whole group of near-finalists was to spend a whole day "on the district", observing and assisting the district nurses at their work. During the morning they cared for patients in their own homes, and here I was instructed how to fold old newspapers to form a basket for waste dressing materials and how to bake wool and gauze in a biscuit tin with perforations to sterilise the contents. The afternoon was spent in a local community hall at a baby and toddler clinic, assessing the development and watching vaccination procedures. This was all very exciting as over the years we had become much institutionalised. We certainly saw life and suffering from a different angle and were more aware of where the patients had come from and even more where they were going home to.

Now my extended training was nearing its end and I was putting extra effort into exam preparation. It was at this time that "flu" vaccinations were introduced for carers, and we were all expected to have them. I did, and whether as a result of this or not, I became ill with a high temperature and shivers. For the first time in three and a half years I was not able to report for duty. I was admitted to the nurses' sickbay. This was a small ward attached to the children's ward; the feeling of being "looked after" was very acute, whilst feeling so wretched the warm bed, food delivered on a nicely laid tray, care from the chief physician and peace were a novel experience. Whatever we lacked in salaries we

"NURSE!"
"Yes, Sister?"

were not neglected when sick. I soon recovered and went back to work.

October was soon upon us and then the hospital finals were taken and then the state. Thoughts started turning to what comes next. Being a nurse and not being able to deliver a baby was not a good thing, to our thinking, so a number of us elected to train as midwives. Results came out and happily I was successful, as were most of the group I had joined onto. Culmination came with the final prize-giving and awarding of certificates. The years in training had all been worthwhile; then and now I can look back and be very thankful for the opportunity given to me initially and all the superb teaching I was given from the nurses and doctors and other professionals, which was of the first order.